DOG OWNER'S GUIDE TO THE
Border Collie

Adrienne McLeavy

FIREFLY BOOKS

A FIREFLY BOOK

Published by Firefly Books Ltd. 2005

Copyright © 2005 Ringpress Books Limited

First printing

Publisher Cataloging-in-Publication Data (U.S.)

McLeavy, Adrienne.

Border collie/Adrienne McLeavy.

[80] p. : col. photos.; cm.
(Dog owner's guide)

Summary: A dog owner's guide to the care and training of Border Collies.

ISBN 1-55407-072-4

1. Border collie. I. Title. II. Series.

636.7374 22 SF429.B64M35 2005

Library and Archives Canada Cataloguing in Publication

McLeavy, Adrienne

Border collie/Adrienne McLeavy.
(Dog owner's guide)

ISBN 1-55407-072-4

1. Border collie. I. Title. II. Series.

SF429.B64M34 2005   636.737'4
C2005-900983-7

Published in the United States by
Firefly Books (U.S.) Inc.
P.O. Box 1338, Ellicott Station
Buffalo, New York 14205

Published in Canada by
Firefly Books Ltd.
66 Leek Crescent
Richmond Hill, Ontario L4B 1H1

Printed in China

ACKNOWLEDGMENTS

First of all, I would like to thank my long-suffering husband, Bob, for putting up with me and my dogs for 32 years.

Thanks also to my daughter, Pam Bolus, for reading the manuscript, and to Barbara Swann for introducing me to the Border Collie many years ago. Thank you to John Sellers and Carol Ann Johnson, for providing some really great photographs.

Finally, thanks to the kennel clubs of Australia, New Zealand and Canada.

Adrienne McLeavy

CONTENTS

1 INTRODUCING THE BORDER COLLIE

Dogs were first used by humans as guards against wild animals. Later, they were used to guard homes and livestock.

With humans living in such close proximity to their dogs and livestock, the next progression was to utilize and improve on the dogs' natural herding instincts.

The first reference to the working sheepdog, or Border Collie as we know it today, was in 1570, when Dr. John Caius, Physician in Chief to Queen Elizabeth I, wrote his *Treatise on Englishe Doggess*. Although he describes the work of the Border Collie as answering his master's voice or whistle to bring the sheep or drive them, he does not make any reference to the type of dog, only the ability to work sheep.

Around the 1700s, there were many references to the "Collie"-type dog used by shepherds in Scotland. These dogs were used for working sheep in the hills and mountains of the border counties of Scotland, England and Wales, hence the name "Border Collie" evolved.

BUSINESS PARTNERS

Originally, the Border Collie accompanied shepherds everywhere. The hill shepherd would winter in the lowlands and valleys, working his way up to the hill-tops during the spring and summer. The dogs would be constant companions, guards and working partners, and this close relationship is one of the reasons why the Border Collie adapts to most working partnerships.

All-around Sheepdog

The Border Collie's physical and mental make-up has been developed with one purpose in mind—to herd sheep. If you know how the breed uses its natural instincts, you will better understand your pet Border Collie's behavior, and this will lead to a better relationship with your dog.

The Border Collie works sheep by employing the basic predator-prey relationship, which is controlled by the shepherd. The basic chase instinct can show itself in many undesirable ways in a pet Border Collie, such as chasing cars, joggers and children—to name but a few. For this reason, the instinct must be controlled from a very early age.

THE VERSATILE BORDER COLLIE

The Border Collie has such a strong desire to work and to please that the breed is capable of carrying out most working tasks.

- Competitive obedience: The Border Collie is the number one breed in this sport—he is quick to learn, and thrives on the hours of training needed for precision work.
- Agility: again, the Border Collie is outstanding in this sport, which calls for speed, balance and instant control.
- Flyball: another sport well suited to the breed, Flyball is self-motivating, and also encourages the strong chase instinct.
- Working trials: The Border Collie has made a name for himself in a sport that calls for control, agility and a good sense of smell.
- Search and rescue: Border Collies have come into their own in this activity. The dogs need to work in the hills and mountains in all weathers. To a Border Collie, there is not much difference between searching for a lost sheep or a lost person!
- Guide dogs for the blind: Although Border Collies have been used as guide dogs, the breed's sense of initiative can count against him. A calmer dog, that is not so work-oriented, is generally preferred.
- Assistance dogs: these include dogs trained to assist the deaf or disabled. Border Collies can be suitable for this type of work and, in many cases, initiative is classed as an asset. However, the Border Collie is a very active dog, which can present difficulties for owners with mobility problems.

The Border Collie was bred to work sheep. He excels at all the canine sports and also makes an outstanding assistance dog.

Understanding Initiative

This is a breed that has the ability to work on his own initiative. When rounding up sheep in the hills, he can work two or three miles away from his handler without any commands to follow.

This anticipation and quickness to learn brings its own problems when training the breed. Unless the handler remains one step ahead, the Border Collie will take the law into his own hands. This is why it is so stimulating to train a dog that returns from a task at breakneck speed, as if to say: "Been there! Done that! Now what?"

Breed Recognition

The first Sheepdog Trials were held in 1873 at Rhiwlas Bala, north Wales. In 1906 the International Sheepdog Society (ISDS) was formed. Generally, dogs can only be registered with the ISDS if both parents are

The instinct to work remains strong in the Border Collie.

registered. Each dog is given an individual registration number.

The Border Collie is recognized by the American Kennel Club, but not the Canadian Kennel Club. In Canada, Border Collies can be registered with the Canadian Border Collie Register which is affiliated with the American Border Collie Association.

The term "working sheepdogs" refers to crossbred Collies or Border Collies that have never been registered (or are without any pedigree papers).

THE BREED

The Breed Standard is a written blueprint which describes the "ideal" Border Collie. In the show ring, a judge will use the Breed Standard to evaluate each dog, and it is the dog that, in his opinion, conforms most closely to the Standard that will be placed.

The Breed Standard is approved by a country's national kennel club, and there are minor differences depending on where the breed is being judged.

GENERAL APPEARANCE
The Border Collie is a medium-sized dog, which should show perfect balance and give an impression of endurance.

TEMPERAMENT
Alert, energetic and highly intelligent, with a strong instinct to work.

HEAD
The skull is fairly broad, with the muzzle tapering to the nose. The

STANDARD OF THE BORDER COLLIE

OCCIPUT

WITHERS

CROUP

TOPLINE

STOP

MUZZLE

CHEST

STIFLE

TUCK UP

HOCK

PASTERN

eyes are set well apart, and are brown in color. Blue eyes are a fault, except in merles.

The ears are set well apart, and are carried erect or semi-erect. The teeth and jaws are strong, and the teeth should meet in a scissor bite (the upper teeth closely overlapping the lower).

BODY
Athletic in appearance with a deep chest and well-sprung ribs. The body is slightly longer than

An alert, intelligent expression is typical of the breed.

the height at the shoulders. The forelegs are straight and parallel, the shoulders well laid back, and the elbows close to the body. The hindquarters are broad and muscular.

PAWS

Oval in shape, toes arched and close together.

TAIL

Tail moderately long and set on low. It may be raised in excitement, but should never be carried over the back.

COAT

There are two varieties: moderately long and smooth. In both, the topcoat is dense and the undercoat is soft and weather-resistant.

COLOR

A variety of colors is allowed, but white should not predominate.

MOVEMENT

Free, smooth and tireless.

SIZE

In the United States, the Standard asks for 19–22 in (48–56 cm) for dogs, and 18–21 in (46–53 cm) for bitches. There are no Standard sizes in Canada.

2

THE RIGHT CHOICE

Taking on any dog is a big responsibility. Taking on a Border Collie—a breed with a strong desire to work—needs special consideration.

You cannot expect a Border Collie to settle down to a quiet life, with limited exercise opportunities. The Border Collie needs mental stimulation and plenty of free-running exercise. If you cannot provide this, opt for another breed.

Counting The Cost

Can you afford to keep a dog?

- Food bills: quite a range in price depending on quality.
- Vaccinations: the first program must be followed up with annual booster shots.
- Deworming: this is not expensive, but it must be done every three to four months.
- Vet fees: these are usually charged as consultation fees, with treatments as a further charge.
- Insurance: this offers protection against vet bills. Remember, preventive treatment (vaccinations, deworming, etc.) is not usually covered.
- Boarding kennels: you may need to pay for kenneling if you go on holiday or into hospital, etc.

WHAT DOES THE

- Are all family members keen on getting a dog?
- Who will take overall responsibility for the pet?
- Does your lifestyle suit a very active, working breed?
- Do you have the time for training and socialization?
- If you have young children, can you cope with another responsibility?
- If you have an elderly parent living

Finding A Breeder

The best way to find a Border Collie puppy is to go to a recognized breeder where the litter has been reared in the home. These puppies will be well socialized from the beginning; they will be used to everyday noises, such as the vacuum cleaner and washing machine, and they will be familiar with the comings and goings of family life.

In the United States, contact the AKC for a list of breeders.

In Canada, breeders can be found through the Canadian Border Collie Association, or in *Dogs in Canada Annual*.

If you are looking for a Border Collie for a specific activity, it is advisable to consider particular bloodlines. Some breeders specialize in show Border Collies; others breed for Obedience work; and others breed specifically for working sheep. Breed clubs will provide details of the relevant breeders.

FAMILY THINK?

in your house, is it wise to have an energetic young dog?

● The Border Collie is a quick-moving dog with a strong chase instinct. Will you be able to control your dog?

● The Border Collie has a strong working eye, and is attracted by fast-moving objects—including children running around. Are you prepared to tackle this potential problem?

Many Border Collies are put up for rehoming because their owners could not cope with "problem behavior." If proper consideration had been given to living with an active breed in the first place, the problems would never have arisen.

Take the time to find a recognized breeder who has a reputation for producing sound, typical Border Collie puppies.

The male is bigger than the female, and may be slightly harder to train.

The next thing to decide is whether you want a male (dog) or a female (bitch). Females are smaller, and they tend to be more tractable and easier to train than males.

Dogs are usually a couple of inches taller, and they are heavier than bitches. Although they can be more difficult to train, dogs do not have the same mood swings as some bitches, who are affected by hormonal changes resulting from their breeding cycle.

A bitch usually goes into heat every six months and, for a three-week period, she must be kept away from males. During this time she will have a discharge

NEUTERING

Unless you plan to breed your Border Collie, I would advise all pet owners to have their dogs neutered. It is advisable to wait until your Border Collie is fully mature. For bitches it is best to wait until she has had at least one season before she is spayed. In males, I believe the best time for castration is around 12 to 18 months, when all the male characteristics are fully developed. Ask your vet for further advice.

FEMALE?

The female is sweet-natured and biddable, but you will have to cope with her seasonal cycle.

—which can make a mess— although most bitches keep themselves quite clean.

Dogs are just as loyal and companionable as bitches. Some may show a tendency to antisocial behavior, such as mounting cushions or visitors' legs. However, if reprimanded at an early stage, there is no reason why it should persist as a problem.

Some males tend to wander, particularly if there is an in-heat bitch in the neighborhood. The best solution is to keep your home and yard secure so your dog cannot stray.

Coat Length

Border Collies come in many coat types ranging from smooth-coated to the really rough-coated.

Personally, I prefer a medium-coated dog, with a dense undercoat and a longer topcoat. This type of coat usually has feathering on the legs and tail, and a ruff around the neck.

This coat offers protection from the cold and wet, but the mud does not stick to it.

If your dog gets wet and dirty, just rub it with a water-absorbent cloth and brush when dry.

COLORS

The traditional coat color is black and white (pictured above).

- The coat is mainly black on the back and head.

- There is a white stripe in the middle of the face.
- There are white markings on the legs and the chest.
- The tail is black with a white tip.

There are considerable variations to this pattern, and some dogs may have white markings on the body. Some may even have a white, or half-white, face.

Red and white: The shade of red can vary.

Red tricolor: A color that is rarely seen.

Blue merle: A distinctive color which has its own enthusiasts.

The other Border Collie colors are:
- black and tan;
- tricolor (black, tan and white, or red, tan and white);
- red and white (the red can be any color from liver to foxy tan);
- blue and white;
- red merle;
- blue merle.

The merle colors are various shades of blue or red, with a marbling effect and black mottling.

OFF WHITE

According to the Breed Standard, white should not predominate. It is generally believed that sheep take less notice of a white dog, although a number of white dogs have disproved this theory and have proved to be good working dogs.

IF YOU CHOOSE AN OLDER DOG ...

Depending on your circumstances, it may be advantageous to take on an older dog.

They are usually housebroken and know the elements of basic obedience. Most will fit into your routine fairly quickly, although it can take a few weeks for the dog to show his true character.

The disadvantage of an older dog is that you are taking on an unknown quantity. Use your common sense and take things slowly until you both have had a chance to get to know each other.

Make sure the dog is given time and space to settle in (especially if there are children in the family). Above all, rescued dogs need patience and understanding.

ASSESSING THE LITTER

When it comes to choosing your new puppy, don't let your heart rule your head. Ask to see the puppies with the bitch, so you can assess the mother's temperament.

Do not fall for the puppy that hides in the corner, as nerves showing at this early stage could store up trouble later in life. At the other end of the scale, the bold, bossy puppy, who beats up all his littermates, could turn into a real handful.

The ideal pup is the middle-of-the-road type, who is involved in all the play and takes everything in his stride.

- Puppies should smell fresh.
- They should be clean, with no evidence of fleas.

- The ears should be clean and pale pink.
- The pups should feel solid when picked up—a light puppy with a distended stomach is almost certainly carrying a worm burden.

If you are looking for a show dog, go to a breeder who specializes in producing dogs with excellent conformation, a mouth with a regular scissor bite, and good markings.

Watch how the puppy moves, as it will give you an idea of how the puppy is made.

For those who want to train in Obedience, choose the pup who is keen to play and retrieve, and likes interacting with you.

Be guided by the puppies' breeder, who will know the litter as individuals. If none of the pups appeal to you, then leave it until another time.

▲ *It is important to see the puppies with their mother.*

▼ *If you want an Obedience competitor, choose an outgoing pup who loves to retrieve.*

HEALTH CHECK

Check with the breeder that the puppies' parents have been tested for Collie Eye Anomaly (CEA) and Progressive Retinal Atrophy (PRA). The parents should also have been x-rayed for Hip Dysplasia (HD). Ask to see the relevant paperwork to be sure of the results. See also Chapter Six.

21

PREPARING YOUR HOME

Sleeping Quarters

In most cases, the puppy will sleep in the kitchen or utility room. It is important that the area is warm, draft-free and safe. There should be no trailing electrical wires—or other dangers—close to the pup's bed.

Beds and Bedding

Do not buy an expensive dog bed, as you will probably get the wrong size for a fully grown Border Collie—and the puppy will have chewed it long before you reach that stage!

The best plan is to provide a strong cardboard box, lined with a blanket. As the pup grows, get a bigger box. When he is around

Wait until your pup has stopped chewing before you buy an expensive bed.

5 to 6 months of age, and you have more idea of his adult size, you can invest in a suitable bed.

Dog beds come in all shapes

WHY AN INDOOR CRATE IS JUST

The main advantage to indoor crates is that you can confine your puppy for short periods when you do not want him underfoot, and it also provides the puppy with a safe haven where he can rest undisturbed. The crate also aids housebreaking, as most puppies will instinctively not soil their own bed.

It should never be used as a punishment, and the puppy should only be confined for limited periods.

and sizes, from quilts and beanbags to wicker baskets and molded plastic beds. Plastic, kidney-shaped beds are easily washed and will last a lifetime. The bed can be lined with suitable bedding. Faux fur bedding, which is machine-washable, is convenient for the owner—and comfortable for the dog.

Collar and Leash

At first, a light, nylon collar and leash will be all that is needed. As your puppy grows, replace the collar with a larger one. It is recommended that all dogs wear a collar with identification.

A rolled, leather collar is ideal, as this snuggles around the dog's neck and does not mark the fur.

Collars and leashes come in a variety of colors and materials— including rope, nylon, webbing or leather. Nylon leashes can chafe the hands, particularly if your youngster pulls. The best option is a leather leash with a strong trigger-hook fastening.

Bowls

Your puppy will need two bowls—one for food and one for water. I use stainless-steel for feeding, and the heavier crockery-type for water. It is important that your dog always have access to clean, fresh water.

THE THING ...

In most cases, the puppy will learn to look on the crate as his "den," and will go into it voluntarily. A crate can also be used in the car, giving your puppy a safe, comfortable place to travel.

Check that the toys you buy can withstand being chewed.

Toys

Puppies and adults will appreciate having toys to play with. Hard, rubber toys are helpful when your puppy is chewing, but check that bits cannot be chewed off and swallowed.

My dogs love to play with a ball on a rope, and a game of Frisbee is fun for dogs and owners alike.

There is also the Kong, a hollow, conical-shaped toy that bounces erratically, and this gives hours of entertainment. Stuff food into the hollow, and your dog will spend ages trying to lick it out. The ideal time to give this is when you have to leave your puppy alone for a short period.

DON'T FORGET THE PAPERWORK

The breeder will usually give you a diet sheet and enough food to cover the first couple of meals. If you are buying a pure-bred Border Collie (as opposed to a working sheepdog), you will also get the paperwork needed for registration. In the U.S., register dogs with the AKC; In Canada, do it through the Canadian Border Collie Register.

Collecting Your Puppy

Arrange for your new puppy to arrive at a quiet time, when you have nothing particular organized for a couple of weeks. Christmas is never a good time to settle a new pup—there is too much going on for a puppy to be able to adjust to his new owners and surroundings.

Collect your puppy early in the day so he has a chance to settle before nighttime.

INTRODUCING THE FAMILY

Your new puppy has a great deal to get used to when he first arrives home, so do not introduce any additional distractions, such as inviting friends and neighbors to see the new arrival. When you get home, take the puppy into the garden, and then introduce the family.

If there are young children in the home, make sure they do not pick up the puppy or play with him unsupervised.

A puppy is not a toy and, while children will get endless amusement from a puppy, they must be taught to respect the rights of another creature.

A puppy enjoys play sessions, but he also needs times when he can rest undisturbed. Children must learn not to pester the puppy at these times or you will end up with a bad-tempered dog.

Equally, the puppy must be taught how to behave with children. This is all part of the responsibility of taking on a dog, and you must be prepared to give

plenty of time to establishing a good relationship right from the beginning.

My dogs are 100 percent trustworthy, but I would never leave them alone with small children.

FELINE FRIENDS (AND CANINE COMPANIONS)

Cats are not usually a problem with puppies. Most cats will usually lie low for a couple of days, and will gradually accept the new intruder on their own terms. Make sure the cat does not feel usurped, and give lots of attention, particularly when the puppy is asleep and not demanding attention.

Cats usually stay high up on the backs of chairs, cupboards, stairs, etc., well out of reach until they are more certain what reaction they will get from the newcomer.

Never let the pup chase or bark at the cat. If the puppy gets away with bad behavior at this age, you have only got yourself to blame when you end up with an incessant barker and livestock chaser when he is older.

- Introducing a pup to an older dog (right) is best done on neutral territory. Take the older dog out to a field or a friend's yard, and introduce the pup. Let them play together before taking them back home, and you shouldn't have any problem.

THE FIRST NIGHT

Your puppy's first night in his new home will always be the worst—every night thereafter will see some improvement. The puppy is going to miss his littermates, and he will feel lonely.

It helps if, a week before you are due to collect your puppy, give the breeder a piece of bedding to put in with the litter. When you collect your puppy—and the bedding—you will be bringing home the scent of the litter. When you introduce your puppy to his new bed, put the bedding in with him and this will provide some comfort.

Remember to be firm if your puppy cries. Most will soon give up when they are tired and, if you give in, you will end up with a puppy that is determined to sleep in your bedroom—or even on your bed!

Make sure the puppy is warm, comfortable and well fed, and he should soon learn to settle.

3 CARE PROGRAM

When you first get your Border Collie puppy, the breeder will give you a diet sheet, stating what the puppy has been reared on.

You should feed the same type of food for a few days until the puppy settles in his new home. If you decide to change the diet, do it gradually, mixing a little of the new food in, taking a few days for a complete changeover to take place.

TRADITIONAL DIET

I feed raw meat and kibble, and my dogs certainly thrive on it. When a puppy is eight weeks old, I feed four meals a day— 8 am, noon, 4 pm and 8 pm. The 8 am and 4 pm feeds are usually milk-based, and the others are meat-based.

Milk Feeds

For the milk feeds, I use a dried-milk feed, which can be obtained from pet stores. It is important to follow the manufacturer's instructions, as quantity is governed by the weight of the pup. I add a teaspoonful of honey to this, as well as some cereal.

Meat Meals

For the noon and 8 pm feeds, I give raw meat with some soaked puppy meal and a variety of vegetables (raw or cooked).

I give about 4–6 ounces (114–117 g) of meat per meal when the puppy is seven to eight weeks old, increasing as the pup grows. The puppy is usually the best guide as to the amount he needs, and you can tell just by looking at him if he is getting enough to eat.

As a general rule, if your dog does not finish his meal, never leave it down—let him wait for the next mealtime. As with some humans, the amount of food each particular dog eats before putting on excess weight will vary.

When the puppy is about 4 months old, I cut out the afternoon milk feed and increase the quantity

of the other meals. At around 10 months old, the dog will be on one meal a day, consisting of about 12 ounces (340 g) of meat and two to three handfuls of good-quality meal, plus a snack in the morning. Meat can be fed raw or cooked. If you are feeding food that has been stored in the fridge, make sure you bring it up to room temperature before feeding.

VEGGIE TREATS

My dogs love to eat a raw carrot after a meal, and I also use a variety of green leaves such as dandelion, parsley, mint, and watercress, as well as raw garlic. These are all beneficial to a dog's health, but they should be finely chopped, almost to a pulp, as dogs have difficulty in digesting cellulose. I add a large teaspoonful of these chopped leaves to their meal.

Complete foods

These are usually sold by the bag, and are in pellet form or flaked. They include all the vitamins and additives your dog requires, and so no supplements should be given.

Manufacturers have formulated different diets to suit a dog's age and lifestyle, such as puppy, adult and working, and there are also diets for overweight and senior dogs.

Follow the manufacturer's instructions for the quantity to feed. Complete foods can be fed dry or soaked in warm water but, if you are feeding dry, ensure that there is a supply of clean, fresh drinking water available at all times.

Canned Meat

There is a tremendous choice of canned foods available and they vary with regard to contents. The cheaper brands may contain a lot of jelly or cereal, so they may not provide a well-balanced diet.

This type of food is usually fed

Complete diets are formulated specifically for age and lifestyle.

mixed with kibble, which can be fed dry or soaked before mixing with the canned meat.

GROOMING

Your Border Collie puppy should get used to being groomed and handled from an early age. Start with a soft brush. At this stage, the puppy's coat does not actually need grooming, but a few minutes' gentle brushing every day will accustom him to the procedure.

As the feathering begins to grow on the legs, tail and chest, comb through the coat to remove any knots. Make sure you check behind the ears, where fur mats often accumulate. After combing, give the dog a good brushing with a stiff brush, then finish off by polishing the coat with a piece of velvet to bring up the shine.

A couple of grooming sessions a week should be sufficient to keep your Border Collie in good condition, although you may need to give daily attention when the dog is shedding his coat.

Another reason for grooming is that it provides an ideal opportunity to examine your dog on a regular basis.

In the summer, keep an eye open for grass-seeds. These stick in the dog's coat and can work their way into the eyes, ears, nose or pads, causing many problems.

BATHING

Bathing dogs on a regular basis removes the natural oils from the coat. However, the need may arise if your dog has rolled in something particularly obnoxious, or if you need to give him an insecticidal shampoo for fleas.

- Make sure you have a good-quality dog shampoo and conditioner.
- Stand your dog on a rubber mat, either in the bath or, ideally, in the shower. This will give him a non-slip surface so he will feel safe.
- Soak the dog's coat in lukewarm water, and then work the shampoo into a rich lather.
- Rinse thoroughly, making sure you get all the shampoo out of the coat.
- Before you allow your dog to leap out of the bath, soak up most of the excess moisture using a towel.
- Make sure your dog is thoroughly dried after the bath, either by toweling or by using a hairdryer on a low setting.

WET, WET, WET!

Remember, after you have bathed your dog, his coat will not be as waterproof as normal as you have washed out all the natural oils. These will return in a week or so, but, in the meantime, if your dog gets really wet in the rain, make sure you dry him well.

HEALTH CHECKS

Your Border Collie should be groomed at least once a week, and this provides an ideal time for a general check-up. If problems are spotted at an early stage, you can often prevent a far more serious condition developing.

As you groom, get to know the feel of your dog by running your hands over him. In this way, you can check for abnormalities or any soreness. Through this contact when grooming, you will soon know if your dog is feeling unwell.

A healthy dog will have a moist, cold nose, clean, bright, alert eyes, a silky coat, and will be lively and attentive. By contrast, a dog that is off-color will often have a warm, dry nose,

the eyes will be dull, and the coat will lose its healthy sheen. If you know what is normal for your dog, you will quickly detect any change in appearance or behavior.

Teeth

Teeth should also be cleaned on a regular basis to prevent tartar accumulating and to keep the breath sweet-smelling. There are a number of excellent brands of dog toothpaste, which can be obtained from your vet or pet store. If you clean the teeth just once a week, it could save your dog from having a major de-scaling later in life, which would require a general anesthetic.

Large marrow bones are excellent for your dog's teeth. The dog enjoys chewing and gnawing

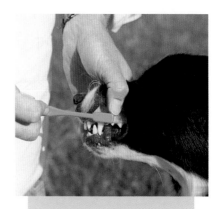

Your puppy will soon become used to teeth cleaning.

at the bone, and this helps to keep the teeth clean. However, it is important to supervise your dog when he has a bone. Never give your dog cooked bones, e.g. chicken or chop bones, as these can splinter and, if a sharp piece is swallowed, it could perforate your dog's stomach.

Nails and Paws

Check the paws for long nails and for cut pads. If your dog's nails have grown too long, they will need to be trimmed (pictured above right). Although most pet stores sell nail clippers, it may be advisable to ask your vet

EARS

Check your dog's ears to make sure they are sweet-smelling, with no brown wax in them. Ear mites can cause a problem, because they irritate the dog so that he scratches continuously at his ear. Parasitic drops, prescribed by your vet, will soon eradicate the mites.

to perform this task, as most dogs dislike having their nails trimmed. Each nail has a "quick" running down the middle. If you cut off too much nail you will cut into the quick, which will bleed, causing pain and discomfort to your dog. If the nail is white it is easy to see the pink quick, so you will know how far back it is safe to trim. In the case of black nails, it is a matter of guesswork. If you are not sure how much nail to cut, just trim a little at a time.

EXERCISE

Puppy

People have differing opinions on the amount of exercise a Border Collie needs. However, it is widely acknowledged that a puppy's exercise should be limited while he is growing. As long as your puppy has access to a fenced yard where he can run free, he will have all the exercise he needs. Try not to let over-enthusiastic children tire your puppy out, for, although a puppy needs exercise, sleep is equally important.

The Border Collie

When you start to exercise your puppy on a collar and leash, bear in mind that this is forced exercise. Your puppy has no option but to walk with you. When your puppy is less than five months of age, do not subject him to mile after mile of hard road-walking. This can prove very hazardous to the developing dog. Equally, do not allow a young pup to jump in and out of station wagons or hatchbacks as this can damage his joints.

Adult

Personally, I do not believe that an adult Border Collie needs a huge amount of exercise. This does not mean that a dog would be happy living in a high-rise apartment and being taken for a walk on a leash once a day. A Border Collie should have a good, free run two or three times a week. It is important to bear in mind that a dog who is bred to work needs mental stimulation as much as exercise.

Find an exercise routine that suits your lifestyle, but do not make it so rigid that the dog cannot adapt to change if, for instance, you are ill and cannot take him out.

Water Babies

Border Collies love to swim, and this is marvelous exercise for muscle tone and fitness in general. My dogs swim once a week at an equestrian swimming pool. Most dogs start off with a very splashy "dog paddle," and it takes time before they learn to glide through the water with hardly a ripple.

Swimming also has a therapeutic value, and controlled swimming is very beneficial for many back and hip problems, as well as for partial paralysis.

One word of warning: always check that it is safe before allowing your dog to swim in a river, a lake, or in the sea. Each holds its own dangers, such as fast-flowing water, undercurrents, or objects hidden beneath the surface, all of which pose potential dangers for your dog. Remember, it is always better to be safe than sorry and, if you think there is any risk involved, do not allow your dog to swim.

TIME ALONE

Do not make the mistake of never leaving your dog alone. Every dog should be taught to stay quietly at home for limited periods. It is important to start this lesson early on, gradually building up the time you are absent, otherwise you will have an overanxious dog who will fret if he is left alone.

4 STEP-BY-STEP TRAINING

Before you start training, you must find a suitable reward. This can be verbal praise, physical praise, food treats or a toy. Interact with your dog and observe which type of reward he responds to most positively.

There is no point in giving an overexcitable dog lots of physical praise—the dog will just get even more excited. Equally, there is no point in training a dog with treats if he has just eaten his meal—he will probably be too full to care!

It is also important to remember that a random reward gives more incentive for your dog to do well, rather than a reward given every time.

Finding a suitable reward is the key to successful training.

HOUSEBREAKING

This will start as soon as you arrive home with your new puppy. The secret is to be on the alert at the following times:

- After every meal,
- After every drink,
- When your puppy wakes from sleep,
- After a play session,
- Every two hours if he has not otherwise relieved himself.

Take the pup out into the yard and go to the area you have allocated for toileting purposes. Use a command, such as "Be clean," and wait with your puppy until he has performed. As soon as he obliges, give plenty of praise and fuss.

Never just open the door and let your puppy into the yard by himself. You need to be with him so he can associate the command "Be clean" with the action of relieving himself, and receive the praise for having done it.

It takes a little longer to train your puppy to be clean through

The intelligent Border Collie will soon get the hang of housebreaking.

the night, as you will be unable to supervise him. The most important thing is to take your dog out into the yard last thing at night. Stay with him until he relieves himself and then settle him in his bed for the night.

In the morning, it is important to take the puppy outside the moment you wake up. If the puppy hears you moving about, he will get excited and will relieve himself immediately.

If you discover that your puppy has had an "accident," do not make the mistake of being angry. The puppy probably relieved himself hours earlier, and will not associate the telling-off with the puddle on the floor.

Some owners are convinced that their dogs know they have done wrong because they look guilty and hide away. In fact, the dog is merely reacting to the telling-off. He is submitting to you, but he has no idea why he is being told off. It is far better to clean up the mess and hope for better luck next time.

The more vigilant you are, the quicker your puppy will catch on to the idea of being clean in the

house. If your puppy is not given the opportunity to make messes in the house, he will soon realize that the business of relieving himself is confined to the yard, so take him outside frequently.

BE RESPONSIBLE

All owners are responsible for their dog not fouling public places, or, if necessary, for picking up afterwards. The best course of action is to train your dog to relieve himself on command (see page 39). The next part of this exercise is training you, the owner, to pick up after your dog. If you are not prepared to do this, you should not have a dog. There are a variety of "poop-scoops" on the market, or you can simply use a plastic bag.

COLLAR AND LEASH

As long as the collar is light and comfortable, the puppy should not object to it.

- If your puppy starts scratching and fussing at the collar, distract him with a game and he will soon forget about it.

- When you are confident that the puppy has accepted the collar, attach a light, nylon leash.

- To start with, just let the puppy walk around with the leash trailing. This should be done only under supervision as the leash might become entangled.

- After a couple of times of trying this, hold the leash.

- Even at this early stage of leash-training, never drag your puppy by the leash, and never let him pull forward. He must learn that you only walk forward when he is by your side.

Make leash-training fun, so your puppy wants to walk with you.

SOCIALIZATION

Between 7 and 14 weeks, your pup is still small enough to be carried, and so you can go out even though the vaccination program has not been completed.

The best place to visit is a busy park. Find a bench and your puppy can sit on your knee, watching all the hustle and bustle of people, children, baby buggies, bikes and buskers. The advantage of this method is that you can give your puppy plenty of reassurance, stroking him and talking to him, while he takes in all these new experiences. I then go to a busy intersection, still carrying the puppy, and stand watching the cars, buses and trucks, giving the puppy a chance to get used to the noise of traffic. It is also a good idea to visit a railway station, or a railway crossing where you can stand some yards from the barrier. Wait for the train to go past, and give your puppy lots of praise and encouragement.

Go To School

Another good place for socialization is outside a school when the children are coming out. The children can meet the puppy, supervised by their parents, and the pup can get

Your pup should be exposed to a wide variety of experiences.

Every dog should be taught
the basics of obedience:
- To walk on a leash
  without pulling.
- To Sit on command.
- To Lie Down on command.
- To Stay on command.
- To Come when called.
- To Stand to be examined
  by a vet or to be groomed.
- To respond to "No" or "Leave."
- To do an Emergency Down
  (which can be a lifesaver).
- To Retrieve.

THE BASICS

used to lots of different people.

Car journeys will also get your puppy used to seeing lots of different sights and, if you start these early, your puppy will soon become a good traveler.

At this age, a puppy should take all these experiences in his stride. Encouragement and praise will reassure him and will also help to establish the bond between dog and owner.

It is also important that your puppy gets used to other dogs,

but be sure that his playmates are fully vaccinated, and limit his exposure.

If your puppy is worried by a new situation, do not make a big fuss or he will think there really is something to worry about. Encourage him with a few words, then reward him with lots of praise and, perhaps, a treat.

43

HEELWORK

I dislike the word "heelwork" as there is a vast difference between competitive heelwork and the pet owner who wants to take his dog for a walk without having his arm pulled out of its socket.

When you take your Border Collie for a walk, it starts in the house when you put the leash on. This should be done quietly with the dog in the Sit position. If you use your leash in the house for training or grooming, you will avoid the automatic association that a leash means a walk, and the resulting overexcitement.

The next stage is walking to the

door. Do not let the dog pull you. If he lunges ahead, take three steps back and start again. Only move one step forward if

INTRODUCING THE SIT

- Hold a treat at the end of your puppy's nose and move your hand upward, slightly over the pup's head.

- As his head comes up for the treat, so his rear end goes to the floor, giving him the perfect Sit position.

- Say "Sit" and, as soon as the puppy responds, give lots of praise and reward him with the treat.

- Continue to ask your puppy to Sit at each mealtime.

Most puppies learn to Sit very quickly.

your dog is at your side. When you get to the door, open it and walk out in front of the dog. If the dog rushes to get through ahead, shut it once more. This should only take two or three repetitions before your dog learns to stand and wait for you to go first. Repeat the same procedure at the gate.

Stop-start

When you get on the sidewalk, the same theory applies. Only move forward if your dog is walking by your side. As soon as he pulls ahead, stop, back up

three or four steps, and bring the dog into the correct position. Then, and only then, should you move a step forward. Your dog will soon understand that he will get nowhere if he pulls.

Command

The command you use for this exercise can be anything from "Heel" or "Close" to "With me;" it does not matter, as long as you are consistent, so that your dog associates the command with the correct position.

When you are out walking your dog, do not nag at him all the time with repeated commands of "Heel;" the dog will just switch off and ignore you. The aim is for your dog to walk with you and, as long as he is doing this rather than pulling, do not correct him if he is a little out to one side or a little in front. However, if the leash becomes tight, the dog must be reminded that you are on the other end.

TEACHING YOUR PUPPY THE DOWN

- Put your pup in the Sit position, kneeling by his side.
- Hold a toy or a treat in your right hand, below the puppy's nose, and move it downward, encouraging the pup to lean forward.
- At the same time, use your left hand to gently press on the puppy's shoulders as he slides into the Down position.
- Hold him gently in place for a few moments before releasing him.
- Do not forget to say "Down" when he is in the correct position, then give him praise and a treat.

STAYING ON COMMAND

Down-stay

The Down-stay is easier to teach than the Sit-stay, especially with Border Collies, as the Down is a natural position for them. In Competitive Obedience, some people will not teach the Down until they have got a steady Sit-stay, otherwise it can encourage the dog to lie down during the Sit-stay exercise.

Never use your dog's name during the Stay exercise, as this is a means of getting his attention, and you do not want your pup standing up during this exercise.

- To start with, leave your dog for a few seconds only, always returning to him and praising him in the Down position.
- If he gets up from the Down position, stop the praise.
- When your dog is steady, you can increase the time you leave him, and you can also increase the distance. Do this very gradually, a couple of steps at a time, or by adding 15 seconds to the time.
- Never increase the time and distance together. If you are leaving your puppy for a longer period, stand nearer to him or, if you increase your distance, cut down the time of the Stay.
- If you do this exercise every day, you will soon have a dog who will lie down and wait where he has been told.

Once you have trained your dog to Stay in this way, never leave him loose outside a store or in the street—it is too dangerous. If he is frightened by something, he will run.

In Competitive Obedience, the dogs must Stay while the handlers are out of sight.

TONE OF VOICE

Say the command "Down-stay" in a firm, confident manner. You must never sound threatening, just be quietly confident. If your pup breaks the Stay and gets up, hold his collar, take him back to the place where you left him, and repeat the exercise.

Sit-stay

When you are teaching the Sit-stay, the same rules apply as for the Down-stay, only this time you start with the dog sitting by your side on a leash.

- Hold the leash up above the dog's head, but do not hold it tight.
- If the dog makes a move to lie down, pull the leash tight and repeat "Sit-stay."
- Once your dog is in the correct position, slacken the leash a little.
- When he is confident, remove the leash.
- Never expect a dog to stay in the sitting position for more than a couple of minutes.

Stand-stay

The Stand-stay is useful for

The Sit-stay is harder to teach, as dogs are often tempted to go into the Down.

grooming sessions, vet visits, and breed shows when the judge assesses the dog.

- Teach this exercise each time you groom your dog.

- Put his leash on, use the command "Stand," and hold him in the Stand position.
- Your dog will soon associate the command with standing still and being handled.
- Progress as you have done with the other Stays, but restrict this exercise to just a couple of minutes so he doesn't become bored.

COMING WHEN CALLED

Start Recall training at mealtimes, calling the pup by name, with the command "Come." If your puppy is with you when you are preparing the meal, ask another member of the family to take the pup away to the other end of the room, and hold him until you give him the command.

Remember to use your puppy's name with the command "Come." When he comes running to you, hold his food bowl, and give the command "Sit." As soon as the puppy is sitting, give him his food and praise him.

Always sound enthusiastic when you call your dog, and reward with lots of praise.

RECALL RETRAINING

A training line can help with Recall problems (such as where an older dog is too easily distracted). A training line is approximately nine yards (8 m) of picture cord, which you can buy from most hardware shops. Do not use a retractable leash for this exercise.

- When outside in an open space, attach one end to your dog's collar and let the line just drag on the ground behind the dog.
- When the dog is distracted by a scent on the ground, walk to the free end of the line and stand on it.
- Call your dog's name, with the command "Come."
- If he ignores you, pick up the line, and jerk it.
- When the dog returns to you, bend down, give him a treat and lots of praise.

Do not remove the training line when out free-running your dog unless you are 100 percent sure that you can get your dog to return to you when you call him.

HOW TO TEACH YOUR

This command (it does not matter which word you use) means: "Stop doing what you are doing, now!" I teach this when the pup is about 5 months old.

- Sit in a chair, with the dog in front of you, and give him a couple of treats.
- Drop a treat on the floor and, if the puppy so much as looks at

EMERGENCY DOWN

This exercise can be a life-saver, as you can stop your dog in his tracks. I do not teach the Emergency Down until the dog is aged 7 to 8 months.

- This exercise should be taught on soft grass, as the dog should be dropping into the Down in one swift movement.

- Start with the dog on your left side, walking on a loose leash (held in your right hand at hip height).

COLLIE "NO" OR "LEAVE"

the floor, say "No," and, at the same time, pick up the treat.

- Repeat this, giving the dog a few treats, then drop one on the floor.

- In most cases, by the third time, the dog has learned that a dropped treat is not automatically his, and that "No" means "stop what you are doing."

- When the dog is least expecting it, give the command "Down." Move your right hand across your body toward the dog's front, and pull the leash forward and down.

- Press down on the dog's shoulders with your left hand and, if you have completed this maneuver correctly, the dog should drop to the ground like a stone.

- As soon as the dog is in the Down position, immediately praise him and have a play as a reward.

THE RETRIEVE

This exercise can be taught to a young pup through play, but many owners inadvertently teach their dogs not to retrieve. The most common scenario is that the pup picks up something he shouldn't have, the owner runs after the pup, shouting at him and telling him to leave it. If the owner catches the pup, the article is yanked out of his mouth and the pup is given a good telling-off.

Think about what has just happened: as far as the pup is concerned, he has been shouted at for picking something up, and the fuss died down as soon as he dropped it.

Turn this negative situation into a positive one. If your pup picks up something and runs off with it, bend down and encourage the pup to come to you. In this way, the pup will come running to you with whatever he has, and you can give him his reward, be it a treat (all good dog people carry treats

The basis of Retrieve training is play, and this can start at an early age.

in their pockets!) or a toy, and have a play. You have started to teach the pup to bring things to you for a reward, and this is the basis of a Retrieve.

Timing

You might think the pup needs telling-off for picking up a forbidden article in the first place, but you have already missed your chance as the pup will associate the telling-off with carrying the article—not picking it up. Once the pup runs off with the item, all you can do is to turn the situation to your advantage, getting the pup to bring the article to you, and so receive a reward.

- Start play-retrieving by sitting in a hallway or a confined area, so that the puppy cannot run off with the toy or ball.
- Use a small, knotted ball on a rope and just play with the puppy, throwing the ball for him.
- Once the pup has fetched it, have a nice game of tug and then throw the toy again.
- Do not give a lot of commands at this stage—just treat it like

Command "Wait" and throw the dumbbell.

Send your dog with the command "Fetch."

Your dog should return with the dumbbell and present it.

play. When the pup picks up the ball, say "Hold," in a very light-hearted manner so that the puppy starts to associate the command "Hold" with having an article in his mouth.

- For an older dog, use a light training line, as with the Recall, so you can guide the dog back to you with the article, and so stop him running off with it.

- To get a dog interested when he has shown no incentive to retrieve (probably because he has been told off for picking up forbidden objects when he was a pup), use a lot of play and tug games. Do not introduce any formality into these games until your dog is eager to fetch. Then

Use a favorite toy to encourage your dog to retrieve.

you can start telling your dog to sit and wait while you throw the article, and then send him out on the command you want to use.

TRAINING TIPS ...

- Keep your training sessions short: only about five minutes at a time with a young pup, increasing to 10 or 15 minutes.
- Only train when you are in a good mood. Never train when you are tired or irritable, as you will pass these vibes to your dog.

TRAINING TIPS ...

- Keep your dog interested and happy while training, making sure training is not dull or boring.
- If your dog does what you asked of him the first time, never try to do it again right away. The chances are that he will not do it as well, and so you are far better to have left it with his first good effort.

ASSOCIATION TIME

A lot of people get confused when they start dog training, as they seem to be praising their dogs one minute and correcting them the next.

The easiest way to explain this is by association time; the time it takes for a dog to associate the command "Sit," for example, with the action of putting his rear end on the floor and receiving the praise for this action. If these three phases—command, action, reward—are completed within a very few seconds, then the dog has a better chance of associating the command with the action and with the praise.

The same applies when you reprimand your dog. Unless you catch your dog at the exact time he is doing something wrong, it is a waste of time telling him off.

TRAINING TIPS ...

● Be consistent with your training. Dogs can understand "Yes" and "No," but do not expect them to understand "Sometimes," "Perhaps" or "Maybe." It is not fair to let your dog jump up on your knee when you feel like a cuddle, then to discipline him for jumping up on a guest's lap.

5 THE WORKING INSTINCT

For generations, the Border Collie has been bred to work.

If they are not given the opportunity to fulfil this overriding desire, it can lead to behavioral problems, and you could end up with a very unhappy, neurotic dog.

This is why mental stimulation is as important as physical exercise. If you just exercise your Border Collie, you could end up with a canine athlete bursting with power, but with nowhere to channel that energy!

The chase instinct in some Border Collies is so strong that, if he is not given the opportunity to use this working ability, he could end up chasing sheep, cats, birds, children, bikes, joggers, cars, or even shadows.

FUN AND GAMES

A few simple games will help to keep your Border Collie's mind occupied, and you will also enjoy the fun of playing with your dog.

The following games can all be taught to a dog who has been trained to do a confident Recall, Retrieve, and Down-stay (see Chapter Four). Begin teaching these games when your dog is about 9 to 10 months of age.

At first these games should be easy, gradually increasing in difficulty. Use a different command for each exercise so as not to confuse the dog.

If your dog fails at any part of an exercise, go back a stage and examine your methods. Did your dog fully understand what was expected of him? If the dog gets something wrong, it is usually the fault of the owner. Keep your training fun so that you both enjoy each other's company.

The Border Collie needs both mental and physical exercise.

TEACHING THE DROP ON RECALL

- Leave your dog in the Sit or Down position, give him the command to Stay, and walk away.

- Do not go too far at first; you can increase the distance later.

- Turn around to face your dog, call him to you, but, when he is halfway back, give the command "Down," seeing how close you can drop him to a predetermined spot, e.g., a clump of grass or a bush.

- When your dog has gone down, recall him to you and give him lots of praise and play as a reward.

This exercise should not be overused. It uses the Emergency Down, so you do not want your dog to become bored with it, to the detriment of an instant response in a real emergency.

The exercise also has a tendency to slow down the Recall.

HIDE AND SEEK

This is a great game for playing with other members of the family when you are out on a walk, especially in a wooded area.

- One person should hold the dog and cover his eyes, while the other family members hide.

- Then see how quickly your dog can find everyone.

- Again, start by making it easy until the dog understands what is expected of him.

This game can also be played at home.

- Shut your dog in the hall, and then hide his toy or a treat in another room.

- Make sure the object is quite easy to find, with part of it visible to the dog (e.g., half under a corner of a mat).

- Let the dog into the room, and ask him to "Find" or "Seek."

- When the dog finds the article, give lots of praise. If you have hidden a treat or a chew, he will already have his reward!

- You can make this exercise more difficult as you progress.

FIND THE TOY

- Throw a toy into long grass and send your dog to find it.

- Start by letting your dog see you throw the toy but, as you watch your dog use his nose—not his eyes—to find it, you can begin making it harder.

- Try hiding the toy without your dog seeing, and then send him to find it.

SEEKBACK

This exercise is useful if you accidentally drop something while you are out on a walk—such as your keys or a glove—you can send your dog back to find it!

- Walk along holding your dog's toy, keeping your dog on a leash.

- Drop the toy, allowing your dog to see what you have done.

- Carry on walking for about 12 yards (11 m), keeping the dog's interest by saying, "Where is it?"

- Then turn around, facing toward the toy.

- Release your dog, using the command "Where is it?" and off he should go to find his toy.

- When he returns, make a big fuss of him and let him have a couple of throws of the toy or a game of tug.

- Increase your distance, and get your dog to go back 100 yards (90 m) or more.

- You can also make it more difficult by not letting your dog see where you have dropped the toy.

IN LONG GRASS

- Make a mental note of where you hid the toy so that, if your dog fails to find it, you can guide him a bit nearer to it, and help him to succeed.

- Always carry a second toy— if the dog loses interest, you can drop it in an easy place while he's distracted. Then he will find it and the exercise will end on a success.

BEHAVIORAL PROBLEMS

In a book of this size, it is impossible to cover the subject in depth, but there are a few guidelines to consider in training. First and foremost, prevention is better than cure:

- DON'T let your Border Collie chase after anything other than an article that can be controlled by you. Control must be incorporated into the games you play with your dog that involve any element of chasing.

- DON'T let your dog play chasing games with children. The only way a dog can stop a child running away from him is by using his teeth.

- DON'T let your 8-week-old pup guard food or possessions. If he gets away with this behavior now, think how he will react when he is a mature dog of 18 months.

- DON'T let your pup get overexcited at the sight of his leash in anticipation of a walk. Use a leash in the house and yard for training and grooming.

Never allow your Border Collie to chase, unless you have thrown a toy for him.

- DON'T let your pup associate the car with the excitement of having a walk. Go for car trips when the dog is never taken out of the car, interspersed with journeys that incorporate walks.

TROUBLE-SHOOTING

Most problems with inappropriate behavior arise because owners are inconsistent in their training. Make sure you are always firm, fair and consistent—and your dog will soon get the message.

Then your dog does not know what to expect.

- DON'T let your pup bark for food, or when excited in anticipation of a walk or game.
- DON'T let your dog dictate to you when he wants to go for a walk, to be fed, or wants to play. You are the one who invites all these interactions.
- DON'T inadvertently praise any sign of nervous behavior. It is all too easy for an owner to be overprotective, reassuring a puppy so much that he feels unable to cope on his own and becomes increasingly nervous and neurotic.
- DON'T let your pup be with you constantly. Make sure he

spends a short period of time in a room by himself.

- DON'T allow your dog to beg for food at mealtimes.
- DON'T allow your dog to rush through doorways ahead of you.
- DON'T allow your dog to bite the brush when you are grooming him.

Don't allow your dog to become overexcited in the car.

*Prevention is better than cure. Keep your Border Collie busy,
and he won't have time to get into trouble.*

- DON'T allow your pup to jump up at you. Ignore him unless his feet are on the ground.

- DON'T allow your pup to walk along the sidewalk without a collar and leash.

KEEP HIM BUSY... AND OUT OF MISCHIEF

If a dog is not allowed to get into bad habits, you will not have to tackle the far more difficult task of correcting bad behavior.

Remember: a bored Border Collie is very likely to become a deviant Border Collie. The working instinct must be channeled in a constructive way so that the dog feels stimulated and motivated.

If his mind is occupied in this way, he will be happy to accept the limitations you impose on his behavior, and he will be the ideal canine companion that you crave.

If you are not prepared to work with your Border Collie, choose a breed that makes fewer demands.

COMPETITIVE DISCIPLINES

The Border Collie excels in all the canine disciplines, and part of the fun of owning this breed is training your dog in a specialist activity. In some cases, such as Sheepdog Trials, this is neither practical nor desirable for the average pet owner. If your dog is not going to work sheep on a regular basis it is far better not to develop the instincts involved, as this will almost certainly cause problems in everyday life.

However, there are plenty of other activities that you and your Border Collie can do.

Sheepdog Trials

Many people think the Border Collie has an inborn instinct to round up sheep and bring them back to the farmer without any training whatsoever! In fact, the Border Collie is, potentially, one of the worst sheep-herders. An untrained Border Collie chases sheep because of the predator-prey relationship—an overriding instinct to chase anything that moves. It takes many months of training to get a dog to work sheep, and it takes years to reach the standard demanded in the top Sheepdog Trials.

Those that are dedicated to competing in this field either keep their own sheep specifically for training their dogs, or have ready access to sheep. This must be coupled with a thorough, working knowledge of sheep.

The lift: this is the dog's first moment of contact with the sheep.

- A Sheepdog Trial consists of an outrun, where the dog is sent out to the left ("Come-by") or the right ("Away to me") of the handler to lift the sheep, which are positioned at the top end of the trial course.

- The dog has to bring the sheep, at a steady pace and in a straight line, through gates to the handler, around the handler, and then drive the sheep back up the course.

- The dog then has to turn the sheep and drive them across the course and into a shedding ring. Here, the handler, with the help of the dog, has to cut out a couple of the marked sheep from the shedding ring.

- The dog then has to gather the rest of the sheep and pen them, all within a set time.

- Points are awarded for the different sections of the course, and the dog and handler with the highest marks win.

Breed clubs will provide details of where trials are being held, or who to contact for further information.

The dog must separate the sheep into two groups.

The sheep are gathered in a tight bunch, ready for penning.

The sheep must be driven into the pen.

AGILITY

The Agility course is made up of a series of jumps, rigid and collapsible tunnels, and weave poles, plus contact equipment (A-frame, a dog walk, a see-saw).

Teaching the dog to negotiate the obstacles is the easy part of Agility; the hard part comes in keeping the dog under control, and going in the right direction, at fast speed, around the course.

More and more clubs are catering to Agility, and there are also a number of weekend and weekly courses. Although this is a

The weave: The Border Collie can negotiate the weave poles at an amazing speed.

highly competitive sport at the top level, it is great fun to take part in at all levels.

Border Collies, who are naturally quick and agile, excel in this discipline and, perhaps most importantly of all, they clearly love doing it.

A-frame (below) and dog walk (right): control and accuracy is needed for the contact equipment.

FLYBALL   IS FUN!

This is another sport that the Border Collie excels in. Unlike all the other dog sports where the outcome is decided by a judge, Flyball is decided by the speed of the team. You either win or lose, and that is that. Dogs really enjoy Flyball racing as it is self-motivating. A team of four dogs have to race over four low jumps to a Flyball box. When a pedal is hit by the dog's front paws, a tennis ball is released. The dog then catches the ball and returns over the four jumps, allowing the next dog to go, and so on until all four dogs have completed the course. The course is 51 feet (16 m) long. Races are started by starting lights, and electronic timing equipment is used to decide the outcome of races.

COMPETITIVE OBEDIENCE

Today, this discipline calls for precision working, and can be compared to dressage in the horse world. This means that many of the breeds that used to compete 40 years ago do not lend themselves to such precise work, so now the Obedience scene is dominated by Border Collies, working sheepdogs, German Shepherds and Retrievers. Other breeds do compete in Obedience, but they are the exception rather than the rule.

The format may vary slightly from country to country, but the

67

basic format remains the same. Handler and dog have to perform a series of exercises in each class, gradually increasing in difficulty as you progress through the classes.

The exercises include Heelwork on and off the leash, Recalls, Retrieves, Sendaways, Distance Control, Scent Discrimination, and Sit-, Stand- and Down-stays. Points are awarded for each exercise, and any mistakes made by dog or handler will lose points.

The handler gives the dog a scent (left). The dog must then find the cloth that carries that scent (below).

TRACKING

Tracking competition allows dogs to demonstrate their natural ability to recognize and follow human scent.

There are two tracking titles: Tracking Dog (TD) and Training Dog Excellent (TDX). A dog earns TD by following a track laid by a human up to 2 hours earlier, along a 400–650 yard (360–600 m) track. TDX is earned by following a trail laid down 3 to 5 hours earlier, along an 800–1000 yard (730–915 m) track; a cross track is laid by a different person, and the dog must ignore this second track.

Both the United States and Canada offer TD and TDX. There are some differences in rules and distance, but the basic principles are the same. Tracking can be done on grassy or dirt fields, and the dog may have to cross standing water to continue the trail. In the United States, variable surface tracking (VST) events are all also offered. A VST dog must demonstrate the ability to follow a 3- to 5-hour-old track through an urban environment (i.e., streets, buildings or parking lots).

BREED SHOWS

At breed shows, dogs are judged on beauty, conformation and movement. In the United States, the AKC hold breed shows. Because the Border Collie is not registered in Canada, there are no breed shows. As a working dog, it is only judged on its ability (i.e. sheepdog trials).

6

GENERAL HEALTH CARE

The Border Collie is a hardy breed and, with common sense and attention to detail, visits to the vet can be kept to a minimum.

However, all owners should be aware of some potential problems which may arise.

External Parasites

TICKS

A tick is a brown insect about the size of a baked bean. They are often found on the head, chest, neck and shoulder area. They attach themselves by their mouths, and feed by sucking the dog's blood. Never pull a tick off as the head will usually be left buried in your dog's skin, which can cause an abscess. Your vet can provide a suitable treatment.

Lyme disease (transmitted by deer ticks) is a serious disease in both dogs and humans, and preventive measures should be taken.

LICE

These are tiny, brown insects that tend to gather around the dog's neck and ears. These can be dealt with using a spray preparation; your vet will advise you.

FLEAS

These small, brown insects cause tremendous irritation to the dog.

They are usually found on the neck and head area, or the base of the tail or stomach. You can often find flea droppings on the skin, even if you cannot see the fleas. The droppings are like black grains of sand.

There are many flea preparations on the market, so ask your vet to recommend a suitable treatment. As well as treating the dog, you must also treat your home.

Spot-on treatments are an effective way of controlling fleas.

INTERNAL PARASITES

Puppies should be dewormed for roundworms, before and after they leave the breeder. Tapeworms, whipworms and hookworms are also common problems. Heartworm can be fatal to dogs and is endemic in parts of the United States and Canada; ask your vet to test your dog and recommend an appropriate preventive treatment.

THE NEED FOR VACCINATIONS

Puppies are routinely vaccinated against distemper, hepatitis, parvovirus and parainfluenza. Vaccinating against leptospirosis is also recommended in areas where the disease is endemic. Vaccination against rabies is compulsory in Canada and parts of the United States. Kennel cough is highly contagious, and can also be vaccinated against. You should keep your puppy away from other dogs until it has sufficient protection; talk to your vet about when the vaccinations will take effect.

CANINE AILMENTS

Allergies

Dogs can become allergic to any number of things: wool, grass, dust, food, etc. In many cases, the skin is affected, becoming red, sore or itchy.

Treatment involves identifying the cause of the reaction, and then removing it from your dog's environment—which is usually easier said than done. Your vet may prescribe anti-inflammatory tablets or give shots to alleviate the condition.

Anal Glands

These are situated beside the anus. Problems can occur if the sacs do not empty when the dog defecates. The sacs become impacted with fluid, turning itchy and sore. The dog might bite at his rear end, or drag it along the ground.

Your vet can empty the sacs but, if the problem persists, the glands may be surgically removed.

Cystitis

Cystitis is when the bladder becomes inflamed. The first symptoms are frequent passing of urine, and discomfort when doing so. You should consult your vet for a suitable treatment. It will help if you take a small sample of urine with you. To do this, place a flat dish under the dog, then transfer the urine to a bottle.

Diarrhea

The general rule is to starve the dog for 24 hours, making sure there is a supply of fresh drinking water readily available. When you next feed your dog, give small, light meals of fish or chicken,

with boiled rice, for a couple of days until you are confident your dog is fully recovered.

If the diarrhea persists, or there is blood in it, consult your vet immediately.

Make sure fresh drinking water is always available.

BEWARE OF HEATSTROKE

This is a potentially fatal condition, which occurs all too frequently when dogs
are left unattended in cars. Even on an overcast day, the temperature inside
a car can build up very quickly. If a dog becomes overheated, the body
temperature must be lowered rapidly, or the dog could die.
The quickest way is to hose the dog with cold water.
As soon as the body temperature is lowered,
take the dog to the vet.

Kennel Cough

This condition is highly infectious
so, at the first sign of coughing,
isolate your dog and consult the
vet. If you take your dog to the
vet's office, do not go into the
waiting room; ask to go straight
into the consulting room. The vet
may prefer to examine your dog
in the car.

Kennel cough usually occurs
where there are large gatherings
of other dogs, such as in boarding
kennels or at dog shows. The first
sign of the disease is when a dog
coughs after exercise or when he
is excited. Owners often mistake
this for the dog having something
stuck in his throat.

Treatment is usually a course
of antibiotics; keeping your dog
warm, quiet and dry will aid
recovery. There are vaccinations
available for kennel cough, and
most boarding kennels will insist
that your dog is vaccinated.

MANGE

There are two types of mange: sarcoptic and demodectic.

Sarcoptic Mange

This can affect a dog at any age, although it is more common in puppies. A parasitic mite lives in the skin and causes irritation to the dog. This, in turn, causes the dog to scratch, which inflames the skin and leads to hair loss. The areas most commonly affected are the muzzle, the ears, the stomach and the legs.

The vet may take a skin scraping for examination. Parasitic washes are usually prescribed to kill off the mites. Remember that sarcoptic mange is highly infectious, so you must isolate an infected dog.

Demodectic Mange

This is not as common as sarcoptic mange, and is usually seen in puppies up to 9 months old. The mite lives in the hair follicles, and bald patches start to appear on the face, chest and legs. Treatment is with parasitic washes and antibiotics. This type of mange is not infectious to other dogs.

STINGS

Try to prevent your dog from snapping at bees and wasps. If your dog does get stung, locate the stinger and pull it out. Then bathe the area with a mild antiseptic. If your dog gets stung in the mouth and it swells up, consult your vet immediately.

Torsion/Bloat

This condition occurs when the stomach swells with gas. The intestine twists, and this can cut off the entrance and exit to the stomach, which keeps on swelling. Immediate veterinary attention will be needed if the dog is to be saved.

To prevent bloat, it is important not to exercise your dog for at least half an hour after he has eaten.

EPILEPSY AND HOW TO DEAL WITH IT

Although this condition is not always hereditary, it is found in some family lines.

Seizures usually occur when the dog is resting or sleeping. The dog will lose consciousness; there will be involuntary movements of the legs in a paddling action, and the jaws may move (as though the dog is snapping and drooling). The dog may also lose control of his bladder.

Although this can be very distressing for the owner, the dog does not know anything about what is happening.

Most seizures last for about 30 seconds to a minute, although it can seem longer at the time. After a dog comes around, a period of hyperactivity may follow, where the dog often bumps into things.

If this happens, try to keep the dog quiet so that he cannot hurt himself. When your dog appears to have

Bloodlines should be researched for evidence of hereditary diseases.

Keep a record of epileptic seizures; this will help to control the condition.

recovered, take him to the vet to be checked over.

Keep an accurate record of the dog's seizures, as this could prove vital when planning the dog's medication program.

EYE CONDITIONS

Progressive Retinal Atrophy (PRA)

PRA is a degenerative condition of the light-sensitive layer of the eye, which can lead to total blindness. The condition is painless and can occur at any age. It is diagnosed by a vet examining the back of the eye with an ophthalmoscope.

There are two types of PRA; Generalized PRA (GPRA), and the type that affects the Border Collie, which is Central PRA (CPRA). Pigmented areas develop over the retina, and this causes loss of detailed vision, eventually resulting in complete blindness. There is no treatment for this condition.

Collie Eye Anomaly (CEA)

This condition is present at birth, and puppies can be eye-tested from 6 weeks. It may affect one or both eyes, and can result in anything from impaired vision to total blindness. In many cases, there may be no noticeable loss of vision, but blindness can occur due to a detached retina. There is no treatment.

Dogs intended for breeding should be tested for CEA, and affected dogs should be excluded from breeding.

It is essential that all dogs intended for breeding are tested for inherited eye conditions.

TESTING TIMES

Breeding stock should be tested for PRA, CEA and HD, with affected dogs (or those with poor hip scores) being excluded from your breeding program.

HIP DYSPLASIA

This condition is found in quite a few breeds, including the Border Collie, and is diagnosed by x-ray.

In mild cases, there may be no obvious sign that anything is wrong, until arthritis develops in the joint in later life.

Severe cases may show in puppies as young as 5 months, with the puppy hardly being able to get up from the sitting position, and having difficulty walking.

Surgery can be of benefit, and some dogs have had successful hip replacements.

OSTEOCHONDRITIS DISSECANS (OCD)

This condition is caused by the degeneration of the cartilage in certain joints. It most commonly occurs in the shoulder joints of some of the larger breeds, but it can also affect Border Collies, and it can appear in other joints.

The condition appears inherited in some lines, but overexercise and oversupplementation have also been attributed.

A puppy may be affected from as young as 4 months, although more frequently between 6 and 9 months. The dog goes lame, which is caused by a piece of cartilage breaking away from the underlying bone. An x-ray will show the problem and, in severe cases, surgery is required.

CARE OF THE VETERAN

At what age does a dog become a veteran? One dog can appear elderly at 8 years old, while others can still be giving a day's work when they are 11. It is now common practice for vets to give dogs aged 7 and over a routine health check when they give the annual booster vaccination.

Feeding times are usually the high spot in any dog's day, and this is particularly true for the veteran dog. It is recommended to feed your dog a lighter diet twice a day, making sure you keep a watch on his weight. Some

complete foods have a senior variety, specifically for veterans.

Grooming is an essential part of veteran care, as this gives you the opportunity to check for any lumps or soreness that may develop. Regular dental care is also vital. Comfort is the key word, so make sure your dog is kept warm, and dry him thoroughly if he gets wet after a walk.

Above all, make sure your oldie feels wanted; never let him feel neglected in favor of a younger dog. Throughout his life, he has tried to give you his best; he now deserves the best care you can give him.